YoungWriters

My First Acrostic

Leeds & Wakefield

Edited by Allison Jones

First published in Great Britain in 2009 by:

 Young**Writers**

Young Writers
Remus House
Coltsfoot Drive
Peterborough
PE2 9JX
Telephone: 01733 890066
Website: www.youngwriters.co.uk

Foreword

The 'My First Acrostic' collection was developed by Young Writers specifically for Key Stage 1 children. The poetic form is simple, fun and gives the young poet a guideline to shape their ideas, yet at the same time leaves room for their imagination and creativity to begin to blossom.

Due to the young age of the entrants we have enjoyed rewarding their effort by including as many of the poems as possible. Our hope is that seeing their work in print will encourage the children to grow and develop their writing skills to become our poets of tomorrow.

Young Writers has been publishing children's poetry for over 19 years. Our aim is to nurture creativity in our children and young adults, to give them an interest in poetry and an outlet to express themselves. This latest collection will act as a milestone for the young poets and one that will be enjoyable to revisit again and again.

Contents

The Poems

Giant Land Snails

Gorgeous snails are really nice.

Interesting snails go round and round forever.

Amazing snails can smell and feel.

Naughty snails eat Keaten's work.

Tiny snails grow bigger and bigger and bigger.

Lovely snails nibble lettuce.

Adorable snails look gorgeous.

Nasty snails are flexible.

Daddy and Mummy love snails too.

Spiral snails have a spiral on their back.

Nasty, naughty snails.

Adorable snails.

It is extremely huge.

Luscious snails are nice.

Slimy snails stick on my hand.

Georgina Procter (7)
Allerton CE Primary School, Leeds

Land Snail

L iving snails on the wall.

A ctive snails when they move all over the place.

N aughty when they eat Keaten's page.

D ifferent when they are born in their white shells.

S lippy because they slither all over the table.

N ifty because they can hide in their shell.

A frican snails like baths.

I nteresting when they eat lettuce with their nibblers.

L ovely when they let you stroke them.

Adam Feaster (7)
Allerton CE Primary School, Leeds

Land Snail

L ives in a tank with other snails
A frican snails love lettuce
N ice, spiral shell with lines
D isgusting, slimy foot under its mouth

S hiny shell on their back
N aughty snails eat paper for food
A nnoying when they look at you
I nteresting body because it's called a foot
L arge shell which is beautiful.

Rachel Chilvers (7)
Allerton CE Primary School, Leeds

3

Land Snail

L and snails move slowly, they have slime under them

A frican snails are bigger than the snails you see outside

N aughty snails sometimes eat Keatan's work

D ad and Mum sometimes stay together

S limy snails slither around slowly

N ice snails eat lots of scrap paper

A ll of the snails slither on the wall

I wish I was a snail

L and snails live in a smelly tank.

Chelsea Wade (7)
Allerton CE Primary School, Leeds

Land Snail

L ovely snails

A nnoying

N ice, beautiful

D elicate

S limy snails

N ice snails

A frican snail's shell is smooth

I f snails are scared they hide inside

L and snails are slow.

Scarlett Taylor (7)
Allerton CE Primary School, Leeds

5

African Land Snail

A snail can share all different feelings just like us.

F ragile snails don't like getting carried.

R eally strong snails carry their baby snails.

I t is scared of lots of people.

C urls its head in if it is frightened.

A dorable snails like getting tickled.

N asty snails hurt your feelings.

L and snails do funny things.

A frican snails are quite big.

N aughty snails do naughty things.

D elicate shells could break.

S lithery snails are slow.

N ice snails like treats.

A lways getting into trouble.

I nside their shell is a slippery body.

L uscious lettuce is their favourite food.

Emily Wood (7)
Allerton CE Primary School, Leeds

6

Snail

S lithery snails like to spread out in the water

N aughty snails like to eat lettuce

A frican snails like sand

I t can hide in its shell

L ettuce to chomp.

Courtney McKenzie (7)
Allerton CE Primary School, Leeds

Snail

S hell is brown and black.

N aughty snail eats Keatan's work.

A ntennae going in and out.

I nteresting snail if you touch the eyes it will go in.

L ong swirly shell.

Sory Keita (7)
Allerton CE Primary School, Leeds

Snail

S nails are extremely slow

N aughty snails eat Keatan's paper

A frican land snails eat lettuce

I t has a shining shell

L ove to slither everywhere.

Rachel Best (7)
Allerton CE Primary School, Leeds

9

Land Snail

L ive in a tank

A frican

N ibbles food

D amp soil

S lithery foot

N aughty snails eat plants

A frica

I n their shells they protect

L and snails.

Joseph Gaunt (6)
Allerton CE Primary School, Leeds

Giant African Land Snails

G orgeous snails slither on my hand

I nside their bodies there are muscles

A ntennae help them to see

N aughty snails eat paper

T wisty snails twist all over

A frican snails always grow

F lexible snails can die if you drop them

R eally hard shells to protect them

I nteresting mouths to munch with

C ute snails have a cute face

A dorable snails sleep in a very smelly tank

N ice snails don't hurt us

L ight as a feather

A lways spread out in the water

N ever naughty

D azzling smooth shells

S lippy foot

N ice snails

A nnoying snails when they look at me

I ntelligent snails because they can see where they are going

L ovely snails tickle me

S nails go inside their shells when you touch them.

Leah Render (7)
Allerton CE Primary School, Leeds

11

Snail

S nails are slimy and slithery

N ice snails like us a lot

A ntennae, they have two

I mportant snails

L ike to eat fish bones.

Juyin Shonubi (6)
Allerton CE Primary School, Leeds

Parents

P roud and happy

A lways there

R ich as a queen

E xcited

N ice food she cooks

T ired

S tories are good at bedtime.

Davina Brazell (7)
Christ Church Upper Armley CE Primary School, Leeds

13

Photographers

P retty photo there

H ot days I take photos

O ut and take a photo

T alented pictures

O utside I took a photo

G reat pictures there

R otten and disgusting photo

A rt pictures are nice

P erfect picture

H er picture is brilliant

E xcellent people in the picture

R ight amazing picture

S mart and handsome photo.

Tanya Chihuri (6)
Christ Church Upper Armley CE Primary School, Leeds

Vicar

V isits our school

I nteresting stories he tells

C hurch is where you see him

A lways kind

R eally hard-working person.

Alex Gilbertson (7)
Christ Church Upper Armley CE Primary School, Leeds

Dhol

D rum made in India

H ard at first to learn

O h! not so hard now but

L oud as loud can be.

Taylor Goodall (7)
Christ Church Upper Armley CE Primary School, Leeds

Bhangra

B hangra dancing

H appy music

A ll can join in

N ot keeping still

G reat to move to

R eally exciting

A ll enjoy Punjabi Bhangra.

Zaynab Hussain (7)
Christ Church Upper Armley CE Primary School, Leeds

Marks And Spencer

M arvellous at all times

A rtistic every day

R esponsible to everyone

K ept going for 125 years

S uper every year

A wesome every week

N ervous sometimes

D elightful at all times

S uperb sevice

P retty clothes they sell

E normous stores

N ice and tasty food

C lever at all times

E xciting inside

R espectful throughout the year.

Amaan Hussain (7)
Christ Church Upper Armley CE Primary School, Leeds

Crazy Dance

C reative in your own way.

R espectful to the visitors.

A rtistic moves.

Z ombie dancing.

Y ear 2 dancing to soft music.

D ancing to the beat.

A cting while dancing.

N ervous the first time.

C omplicated to think of different moves.

E xcited for the people who are watching.

Shanil Ali (7)
Christ Church Upper Armley CE Primary School, Leeds

19

Golden Table

G old is good.

O utstanding food.

L ovely table of food.

D ivine dinners on it.

E xcellent table.

N ice relaxing table.

T able is covered in gold.

A ll the teachers go on.

B eautiful table.

L ike all of it.

E xciting to go on the table.

Rosie Ispan (7)
Christ Church Upper Armley CE Primary School, Leeds

Councillor

C ouncillors are

O kay for everyone

U nderstand everybody

N ice to all

C ouncillors enjoy their work

I nteresting job.

L ocal people they are

L iked by all.

O kay to work with

R eally hard-working team.

Connor Lydon (7)
Christ Church Upper Armley CE Primary School, Leeds

Cohesion

C ouncillor looks after the planet

O utstanding people

H elpful in a respectable way

E qual and sharing

S treet party is a celebration

I nk is in a pen

O pen and honest

N ice girl.

Millie Parsons (7)
Christ Church Upper Armley CE Primary School, Leeds

Handprints

H and full of paint

A nyone can do it

N ice and sticky

D ream for the future

P ainting

R ainbow

I nteresting

N atural

T rees

S ix fingers trailing.

Ashleigh Pilkington (7)
Christ Church Upper Armley CE Primary School, Leeds

Self Portrait

S weet picture

E xcellent activity

L ovely portrait

F ine painting you've done

P retty and neat

O utstanding picture

R osy red cheeks

T rying hard there

R est your body while you're doing it

A n excellent picture of you

I nteresting picture

T reat I will give you.

Jennifer Riley (7)
Christ Church Upper Armley CE Primary School, Leeds

President

P roud

R ich

E nd

S unday

I nteresting

D ay

E vening

N othing to do

T oday, hooray!

Luke Riley (7)
Christ Church Upper Armley CE Primary School, Leeds

25

Community

C ommunities are happy

O utstanding community

M ade handprints

M ade our own faces

U seful for us to learn

N ice place to live

I was impressed

T alk to other people

Y oung and lively place.

Kian Roberts (7)
Christ Church Upper Armley CE Primary School, Leeds

Visitors

V isitors came into the class

I nteresting people came

S ensible talking to us

I nformation things to talk about

T reating people kindly

O utstanding work

R espect people

S pecial things happen.

Preet Sagu (7)
Christ Church Upper Armley CE Primary School, Leeds

Mosque

M orning prayer

O r good

S unday prayer

Q uiet time

U seful

E xciting.

Ahad Shafique (7)
Christ Church Upper Armley CE Primary School, Leeds

Sponsored Walk

S tamp my card.

P eople help me please.

O h no we are walking in rain.

N ice weather.

S ponsor me please.

O n Wednesday we did it.

R un, don't walk

E leanor walk please.

D ig me a hole.

W in me a prize.

A ll are walking.

L isten to Mrs Dhupar.

K eep walking.

Joseph Smith (6)
Christ Church Upper Armley CE Primary School, Leeds

29

Church

C hristians go and pray

H elp, respect people

U nderstanding people

R eligions to pray

C hristians go to church

H elpful in the church.

Jody Sykes (7)
Christ Church Upper Armley CE Primary School, Leeds

Street Party

S amosas were very nice

T reat teachers gave us

R ained outside

E at different kinds of food

E nd was good

T asted very nice

P akoras were very hot

A ll food we tried

R eal fun we had

T una was tasty

Y ummy!

Courtney Woroniuk (7)
Christ Church Upper Armley CE Primary School, Leeds

Enterprise

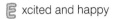

E xcited and happy

N ew shop opening

T his is great

E veryone

R eady

P retty Mrs Dhupar

R eading very

I nteresting book and

S ewing puppets

E nthusiastically.

Umer Rashid (7)
Christ Church Upper Armley CE Primary School, Leeds

The Seaside

S un is very nice to sit in.

E ating in the lovely sunshine is nice.

A t the seaside is fun.

S andcastles are fun to make.

I am enjoying the time at the beach.

D inner was nice.

E ating is always fun.

Luke Foster (7)
Colton Primary School, Leeds

The Seaside

S ea is cold and wet.

E at the yummy food.

A t the beach we swim in the sea.

S and always goes between my toes.

I always have ideas what to play.

D igging for fossils and shells.

E veryone is having fun so let's join in.

Ellis Manson (7)
Colton Primary School, Leeds

The Seaside

S eagulls squeak around our heads.

E verybody is having a fun time.

A fter swimming we can run around on the beach.

S ea is soaking my toes.

I can have a donkey ride.

D igging in the sand for shells.

E ven though we have to go, I've had a super time.

Thomas Casey (7)
Colton Primary School, Leeds

The Seaside

S ee the seagulls squawk above us.

E verybody is in the sea except the lifeguard.

A fter we have played with our buckets and spades
we will have lunch.

S mell fish and chips and salt from the sea and shops.

I can have an ice cream for being good.

D ad tries to park on the beach but I try to stop him.

E ven though we nearly forgot something
we've had a good time.

Harry Emmines (7)
Colton Primary School, Leeds

The Seaside

See the seagulls squawking in the sky

Every day you wish you were there

A donkey is walking up and down

Someone sells seashells by the sea

I can see someone surfing

Drying my sister on the sand

Even when it is time to go home, I wish it was not.

Joshua Cullimore (7)
Colton Primary School, Leeds

37

The Seaside

S ee the sand glittering and gleaming on the sunny beach, what on

E arth is going on? Can we go and join the fun?

A fter tea we're golng homc

S ome time now we're going on a trip.

I need a towel.

D id have a donkey ride.

E verybody's going home so let's go too.

Oscar Reed (7)
Colton Primary School, Leeds

The Seaside

S ee the sea and sand move between my toes

E at the hot dogs and the chips

A t the seaside we look in the rock pools

S ee the seashore with the seashells

I have a candyfloss on the beach

D ig for shells under the sand

E at sweets all the time.

Daniel Gudgeon (7)
Colton Primary School, Leeds

The Seaside

S ee the sunny sand on the land.

E at the food that is sold there.

A t the beach we play games.

S ee the beautiful blue sea.

I eat lots of food and I go on some rides.

D o some shell and fossil hunting.

E verybody's had fun but we have to go.

Andrew James Brook (6)
Colton Primary School, Leeds

The Seaside

S ea goes over my toes.

E verybody is having fun.

A fter swimming I can get an ice cream.

S eagulls are flying around my head.

I want to stay in the sea.

D o some swimming in the sea Mum.

E ven though I have to go home I will come back.

Megan Burke (7)
Colton Primary School, Leeds

The Seaside

S ea, the best seaside ever, every day
you go to the seaside it is the best.

E very sunny day you have got to go
to the beach and play with the sand.

A beach has millions of sandy shells.

S easide is fun because it has lots of things to do.

I can go on the beautiful donkeys.

D o you think the seaside is fun?

E ating lots of ice cream makes me want to have a drink.

Mairi Burrow (6)
Colton Primary School, Leeds

The Seaside

S hells are very ridged.

E ven though we have to go we've had the best time ever.

A t lunchtime I bet we are all exhausted.

S ee all the exciting shops there.

I n the water it is freezing but soon you will get used to it.

D ig, dig, dig for rocks and shells.

E eek go the seagulls above my head.

Aden Manson (7)
Colton Primary School, Leeds

43

The Seaside

S ea is crashing and splashing

E veryone is going to play in the sand

A rcades, we can have fun

S eagulls are squawking above my head

I had some fish and chips

D ive into the beautiful sea

E ating the final ice cream.

Zack Coleman (7)
Colton Primary School, Leeds

44

The Seaside

S eagulls swooping around my head.

E ating ice cream is lovely, I eat it all up.

A fter swimming we can fill a bucket each.

S and and sea coming in my sandcastle.

I n the sea we get very wet.

D addy and me are going to get some food.

E verybody is having a good time.

Laura Keighley (7)
Colton Primary School, Leeds

The Seaside

S ea goes over my toes

E verybody is having fun

A fter swimming we can get an ice cream

S eagulls are flying around

I want to stay in the sea

D o some swimming in the sea Daddy

E veryone had lots of fun.

Sally Jackson (6)
Colton Primary School, Leeds

The Seaside

S ea crashing very loudly, having a picnic.

E veryone is having lots of fun.

A fter swimming we can fill a bucket of sand each.

S and goes in my toes, it tickles.

I can go on the soft sand.

D o some shell hunting.

E verybody's had fun so three cheers!

Ellie Buckley (7)
Colton Primary School, Leeds

The Seaside

S and is messy and it is fun.

E verybody is eating lovely ice cream.

A t the seaside I go in the sea.

S ome time now we are going on a trip to the seaside.

I need a towel because I've been in the sea.

D inner was nice, I had a picnic and an ice cream for pudding.

E very time I go to the seaside I will have an ice cream.

Ellen Louise Hitchman (7)
Colton Primary School, Leeds

The Seaside

S ee the seashells moving in the sea

E at a hot dog and chips while the sea moves

A seagull swoops down while catching its prey

S he sells seashells on the seashore

I eat my ice cream while sitting on my deckchair

D ig, dig for shells

E at lollies while sitting in my deckchair.

Abhishek Tiwari (7)
Colton Primary School, Leeds

The Seaside

S ea is absolutely freezing.

E very day you wish you were going to the seaside.

A t the shop you want a hot dog.

S easide looks beautiful.

I can see millions of shells.

D onkey rides are fun.

E very time I go to the beach it's marvellous.

Sherelle Bennett (7)
Colton Primary School, Leeds

The Seaside

S ee the grainy sand inside your bucket. I'm making
a sandcastle, now I have finished.

E verybody is eating ice cream, quick help,
mine is melting on me.

A t the beach you can surf and play in the sea.

S eashells buried underneath the sand,
come and help me dig for them.

I n the rock pools there are crabs, look closely
and you will find some.

D iving in is scary, just do it and do not think about it.

E very day is lots of fun, come again and have lots more.

Louise Cook (7)
Colton Primary School, Leeds

Our School Poem

F ive lanes is a good school

I like my teacher

V ery good child in school

E veryone is good

L ove my work

A ll children should be good

N ow people are always good

E veryone is great

S chool is great!

Katie Brown (5)
Five Lanes Primary School, Wortley

Our School Poem

F ive Lanes is the best.

I love my friends.

V ery good school.

E veryone is good at work.

L ovely work at school.

A ll the children are nice.

N ow we eat our dinner.

E veryone should be good.

S uper work.

Jacob D'Cruz (5)
Five Lanes Primary School, Wortley

Our School Poem

F reinds are nice at Five Lanes.

I love going to school.

V ery good teachers.

E veryone at school is nice.

L essons are very good.

A t Five Lanes I do good work.

N ice people at school.

E veryone works hard at school.

S chool is great!

Hannah Ergul (6)
Five Lanes Primary School, Wortley

Our School Poem

F ive Lanes is good.

I love it.

V ery good work.

E veryone is good.

L ike the teachers.

A ll nice people.

N ice people.

E veryone is great.

S ave the school!

Alana Hardcastle (6)
Five Lanes Primary School, Wortley

Our School Poem

F ive Lanes rules!

I like Five Lanes.

'V ery good work,' the teachers say to us.

E very day we work as hard as we can.

L ike Five Lanes.

A t Five Lanes the teachers keep us safe.

N ice people at Five Lanes.

E veryone in Five Lanes is nice.

S ome of the children play football.

Fay Hinchliffe (6)
Five Lanes Primary School, Wortley

Our School Poem

F antastic teachers

I love the school

V ery good work

E veryone is good

L earning is fun

A ll the teachers are good

N obody doesn't like me

E veryone likes me

S ometimes people go to the funzone.

Holly May Bailey (6)
Five Lanes Primary School, Wortley

Our School Poem

F ive Lanes is good.

I like my teacher.

V ery good teacher.

E verybody is good at work.

L ike the teachers.

A ll nice people playing.

N ice teachers.

E veryone is lovely.

S ome people go to the funzone.

Emma Banks (5)
Five Lanes Primary School, Wortley

Our School Poem

F ive Lanes is the best.
I t is a good school.
V ery good hot dinners.
E veryone is nice.

L ove my teacher.
A ll do very good work.
N ice people playing.
E veryone loves playing with me.
S ome people go to the funzone.

James Inglis (6)
Five Lanes Primary School, Wortley

Our School Poem

F ive Lanes has nice kids.

I love my teacher.

V ery nice work.

E veryone is nice.

L ove my work.

A ll children should be good.

N ow people are always good.

E veryone is always good.

S uper work.

Leia Izett-Clarke (6)
Five Lanes Primary School, Wortley

Our School Poem

F ive Lanes is the best school!
I like my teacher.
V ery good teachers.
E veryone's nice at Five Lanes.

L ovely dinners at Five Lanes.
A nd the head teacher is brilliant.
N ice dinner ladies at Five Lanes.
E veryone keeps safe at Five Lanes.
S ummer holidays are lovely!

Adam Kellett (6)
Five Lanes Primary School, Wortley

Our School Poem

F riends are nice at Five Lanes.

I like the teachers.

V ery good children.

E verybody is nice to each other.

L ike all the teachers.

A ll children are nice.

N ice to do ICT.

E veryone loves ICT.

S ticking is good.

Zara Madden (6)
Five Lanes Primary School, Wortley

Our School Poem

F ive Lanes is good.

I like school.

V ery good friends.

E verybody is kind to me.

L earning is very good fun.

A t Five Lanes I like my friends.

N ice people come to Five Lanes.

E veryone likes my work.

S ome people go to the funzone.

Kate Naylor (6)
Five Lanes Primary School, Wortley

Our School Poem

F ive Lanes is brilliant.

I love Five Lanes.

V ote for us.

E veryone eats their lunch at school.

L ike my teacher.

A nd our teacher is the best.

N ever let the teacher down.

E veryone is good at Five Lanes.

S ome children are bad!

Charlotte Rafferty (6)
Five Lanes Primary School, Wortley

64

Our School Poem

F ive Lanes is super.

I love Miss Kitchiner.

V ery good school dinners.

E veryone in Five Lanes is good.

L ovely teachers and friends.

A ll children are good in school.

N ice teachers and friends.

E veryone, did you like your work?

S chool is brilliant and good!

Bailey Reed (6)
Five Lanes Primary School, Wortley

Our School Poem

F ive Lanes is the best

I love the children

V ery good teachers

E xcellent work

L essons are very good

A t school it's good

N ice people

E xcellent teachers

S chool is good!

Jake Rollinson (6)
Five Lanes Primary School, Wortley

Our School Poem

F ive Lanes is very brill.

I love Five Lanes.

V ery good work.

E veryone is friendly.

L ove your teachers forever.

A t Five Lanes we do good work.

N ice children.

E ven the teachers are nice.

S ome people are helpful.

Mia Sturgess (6)
Five Lanes Primary School, Wortley

67

Our School Poem

F ive Lanes is lovely.

I think the children are the best.

V ery good school dinners.

E veryone is nice in Five Lanes.

L ovely work at five Lanes.

A very good school.

N ice class.

E veryone does good work.

S afe school.

Lewis Staniforth (6)
Five Lanes Primary School, Wortley

Our School Poem

F ive Lanes is the best
I love Five Lanes
V ery good people
E verybody is nice

L ovely people
A ll children are good
N ice to do PE
E veryone loves our teacher
S pellings are good.

Jack Townend (6)
Five Lanes Primary School, Wortley

Our School Poem

F riends are nice at Five Lanes.

I love all of my friends.

V ery nice teachers at Five Lanes

E veryone is very good.

L ovely work at Five Lanes.

A t Five Lanes we do work properly.

N ice children at Five Lanes.

E veryone's work is a super star.

S ometimes children go home or to the funzone.

Helena Verity (6)
Five Lanes Primary School, Wortley

Our School Poem

F ive Lanes rocks!
I like the teacher.
V ery good work.
E veryone in Five Lanes is good.

L ive in Five Lanes.
A good impression for Five Lanes.
N ice work for everyone at Five Lanes.
E veryone in Five Lanes has good work.
S ee all the good work.

Owen Yarwood (5)
Five Lanes Primary School, Wortley

Our School Poem

F ive Lanes is fantastic

I like Miss Miah she is beautiful

V ote for Five Lanes

E veryone is nice to me

L ovely Five Lanes

A great teacher

N ice children

E ven the teachers are nice

S uper Five Lanes!

Danisha Cowell (6)
Five Lanes Primary School, Wortley

Our School Poem

F ive Lanes rocks.

I love it.

V ery nice teachers are here.

E verybody is fantastic.

L ook for beautiful children.

A big display is up.

N ice and cool in class.

E ven the teachers are nice.

S afe and sound in class.

Lucy Cryer (6)
Five Lanes Primary School, Wortley

Our School Poem

F ive Lanes is the best.

I t's the best school.

V ote for Five Lanes.

E verything is the best in Five Lanes.

L ovely clever children.

A fantastic and clever teacher.

N ice and fantastic Miss Miah.

E verything is the best at Five Lanes.

S uch confident children at Five Lanes.

Lewis Stone (6)
Five Lanes Primary School, Wortley

Our School Poem

F ive Lanes is pretty
I love school
V ery nice school
E veryone is nice

L ovely people in the school
A beautiful teacher in the school
N ice Miss Miah in the school
E very teacher is nice to the children
S unny day when I go to school.

Tegan Germain-Robinson (6)
Five Lanes Primary School, Wortley

Our School Poem

F ive Lanes is in Wortley.

I love Five Lanes.

V ote for Five Lanes.

E verybody loves Five Lanes.

L ovely staff and teachers.

A great and super school.

N ice and cool children.

E veryone goes to great assemblies.

S afe in the playground.

Connor Ward (6)
Five Lanes Primary School, Wortley

Our School Poem

F un Five Lanes

I love school

V ery good school

E veryone is kind

L ovely work

A very nice big school

N ice people

E very teacher is lovely

S unny days when we go to school.

Brandon Aston (6)
Five Lanes Primary School, Wortley

Our School Poem

F ive Lanes is great.

I like it.

V ote for this school.

E verybody is kind

L ovely school.

A great teacher.

N ice school.

E ven the children are nice.

S uper, super school.

Casey Duncan (6)
Five Lanes Primary School, Wortley

Our School Poem

F ive Lanes is super.

I love Five Lanes, it rocks!

V oting for Five Lanes is cool.

E veryone vote for Five Lanes.

L ovely school to be at.

A school that's great.

N ice schools are cool.

E very day the school is clean.

S ensational Five Lanes.

Ella Shaw (6)
Five Lanes Primary School, Wortley

79

Our School Poem

F ancy teachers
I like all the children
V ery nice head teacher
E xtra nice painting

L earning children
A nice teacher
N ice children
E nter Five Lanes
S afe at school.

Ethan Spurling (6)
Five Lanes Primary School, Wortley

Our School Poem

F ive Lanes is a cool school to be at.

I t's nice to be at this school.

V ote for this school.

E veryone in Five Lanes is beautiful.

L ovely school to be at.

A lovely school is Five Lanes.

N ice school to be at.

E very teacher is nice.

S uper duper school is Five Lanes.

Lara Dare (6)
Five Lanes Primary School, Wortley

Our School Poem

F ive Lanes is beautiful

I love it here.

V ote for Five Lanes now.

E at healthy today.

L ove Five Lanes.

A great teacher we have.

N ice teachers.

E ach child is nice.

S end nice messages to each other.

Alec Hubbard (6)
Five Lanes Primary School, Wortley

Our School Poem

F ive Lanes is nice
I love Five Lanes
V ery nice Five Lanes
E veryone is nice

L ovely teachers
A ll the children are great
N ice people at Five Lanes
E veryone is friendly
S ometimes people are funny.

Bethany Hemsley (5)
Five Lanes Primary School, Wortley

Our School Poem

F riends, I play with them

I like Miss Miah

V ery friendly

E ach day I do work

L ike to play out

A sk a dinner lady

N o one is naughty

E nd up happy

S end you home.

Rosie Hargrave (5)
Five Lanes Primary School, Wortley

Our School Poem

F antastic Five Lanes.

I love Five Lanes.

V ote for Five Lanes.

E veryone is kind.

L ovely Five Lanes.

A great caretaker.

N ice children.

E veryone is kind and friendly.

S end a vote to Five Lanes.

Jamie Rooney-West (6)
Five Lanes Primary School, Wortley

Our School Poem

F ive Lanes is beautiful.

I love Five Lanes.

V ote for everyone in Five Lanes.

E veryone is kind and lovely.

L ovely five Lanes.

A lovely school every day.

N ice and sensible school.

E xcellent is Five Lanes.

S uper duper Five Lanes.

Ebony Lawson (5)
Five Lanes Primary School, Wortley

Lion

L ions have shiny teeth

I n the wavy grass

O nly boy lions have a mane

N ow lion's resting.

Marcus Claxton (5)
Garforth Green Lane Primary School, Garforth

Lion

L ions like to lick

I t likes to eat meat

O nly girl lions have babies

N ow the lions are asleep.

Emma Blackburn (6)
Garforth Green Lane Primary School, Garforth

Africa

A frica will be a lovely place to live and have a holiday

F lowers are lovely

R ainforests are in Africa

I n Africa there are lots of animals

C heetahs are the fastest animals in Africa

A frica has 53 countries.

Daisy Turner (7)
Garforth Green Lane Primary School, Garforth

Africa

A frica is the hottest country

F eel the soft animals

R hinos can run very fast

I can see a fierce lion

C reeping lion walking slowly on the grass

A frica has 53 countries.

Ben Lockwood (7)
Garforth Green Lane Primary School, Garforth

Kadeem

K adeem is kind

A musing

D elightful at playing

E xcellent at football

E ntertaining

M agical at handstands.

Kadeem Sage-Morton (7)
Hillcrest Primary School, Leeds

Jade

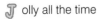 olly all the time

Always sensible

Doubling big numbers

Eats big dinners.

Jade Brown
Hillcrest Primary School, Leeds

Ruhel

R uhel is a kind person

U nusual

H appy all the time

E xcellent at writing

L oving everyone.

Mohammed Ruhel Islam (7)
Hillcrest Primary School, Leeds

Ajhani

A mazing at maths

J olly in the playground

H elpful to other people

A lways working hard

N ice to some kids

I ncredible at dancing.

Ajhani Evans (7)
Hillcrest Primary School, Leeds

Sanaah

S ometimes I am wonderful

A ttractive person

N ice to others

A mazing at badminton

A mazing at washing

H elpful at washing.

Sanaah Raani Nawaz (7)
Hillcrest Primary School, Leeds

Rafey

R aisins are yummy

A mazing at maths

F ruit is my favourite

E njoy playing

Y ellow is my favourite colour.

Abdul Rafey Syed (7)
Hillcrest Primary School, Leeds

Samiha

S pecial friends with

A zizah

M y favourite fruit is strawberries

I am kind

H elpful to friends

A nd my teacher.

Samiha Hasan (7)
Hillcrest Primary School, Leeds

Naqeeb

N ice to my friends

A nd great

Q uick at talking

E very day playing football

E at every day

B eautiful and brave.

Naqeeb Hussain
Hillcrest Primary School, Leeds

Abdul

A m good at maths

B ad at badminton

D elightful at cheering people up

U nderstanding

L ike doing PE.

Abdul Rahman (7)
Hillcrest Primary School, Leeds

Jama

 oyful

A ctive in sports

M arvellous at maths

A lphabet is easy.

Jama Ismail Ibrahim (7)
Hillcrest Primary School, Leeds

Hafiq

H afiq is my name

A lways friendly

F amily is very important to me

I like to play football

Q uick running is what I do.

Hafiq Wan Huzaini
Hillcrest Primary School, Leeds

Roundhay Park

R unning in Roundhay was fun

O n the grass was fun

U sing the tennis racket

N ice and tidy in Roundhay

D oing the parachute was noisy

H aving a big park

A t the park it was fun

Y ear 1 walked to the park

P laying with Bevan was fun

A t the park we went to tropical world

R olling down the hill

K eep the park tidy.

Jessica Long (6)
Moortown Primary School, Moortown

Roundhay Park

R oundhay Park is fun

O n the grass we play

U nder the trees

N ow we are running

D ogs are barking

H ey, we're running

A t lunchtime we ran around

Y oung teenagers were running around

P eople are running around

A nd round the trees

R unning around keeps you fit

K eep the park clean.

Harry Boulton (5)
Moortown Primary School, Moortown

Roundhay Park

R unning in the park

O ver the hills there were trees

U p and down the hills

N oisy children in the park

D o you want to go?

H ave you been to the park?

A round the park there are trees

Y ou have to go to the park

P ark is noisy

A nd we play football

R oundhay Park is fun

K ind people in Roundhay Park.

Amit Rathour (7)
Moortown Primary School, Moortown

Roundhay Park

R oundhay is fun

O ver the hills and down

U p the hills

N ow we are going to the park

D ogs are in the park

H ow did you get there?

A t the park we play

Y o! I'm a boy

P eople in the park

A t the park I play

R ound the trees we go

K eep having fun!

Bethany Whitelaw
Moortown Primary School, Moortown

Roundhay Park

Ⓡ unning around in Roundhay Park

Ⓞ ut in the fresh air

Ⓤ sing the park

Ⓝ othing to put me off

Ⓓ ogs have footprints in the park

Ⓗ ave fun in the park

Ⓐ nd enjoy the playground

Ⓨ ou have to watch out for dog poo

Ⓟ lay nicely

Ⓐ ll around us is plants

Ⓡ unning to keep everyone fit

Ⓚ eep the park tidy.

Arjun Singh Olak (6)
Moortown Primary School, Moortown

Roundhay Park

R oundhay Park is the best.

O ver the hills.

U p and down the hills.

N othing to put me off.

D ogs barking in Roundhay Park.

H aving fun in Roundhay Park.

A t Roundhay Park we played the parachute.

Y our children had so much fun.

P laying in the park is fun.

A t Roundhay Park we had our lunch.

R oundhay Park is my favourite park.

K eep Roundhay Park clean.

Loraine Tumalan-Schumann
Moortown Primary School, Moortown

Roundhay Park

R oundhay Park was fun.

O ur school went to Roundhay Park.

U sing the swings was fun.

N othing to put me off.

D oing the monkey bars was fun.

H aving lunch was yummy.

A t the park we played games.

Y ummy lunch.

P art of it was fun.

A t the park we played with the parachute.

R oundhay Park was fun.

K eep the grass tidy.

Tom Cooper (6)
Moortown Primary School, Moortown

Roundhay Park

R unning at the park is fun.

O ver the hills and trees.

U p and down, jumping all around.

N ice and tidy.

D ogs are walking.

H ave you seen any birds?

A t the park you can run.

Y ou can play a lot.

P lay at the park.

A t the park I can be friendly.

R un and keep it safe.

K eep the park clean.

Yasmin Albaker (6)
Moortown Primary School, Moortown

Roundhay Park

R unning through the grass

O n the grass

U p and down the hills

N ice and clean park

D ogs walking at the park

H ave lots of fun

A t the park there were lots of trees

Y oung kids play at the park

P layground is fun

A t Roundhay Park we had our lunch

R oundhay Park is fun

K eep away from the animals.

Koujiro Tanaka
Moortown Primary School, Moortown

Roundhay Park

R un in the park.

O ver the hills.

U p and down the hills.

N ext had lunch.

D ogs were barking.

H ow did you get there?

A ll around Roundhay Park there were green trees.

Y oung children walking around.

P laying in the park.

A ll around green grass.

R unning around to keep fit.

K eep the park clean and tidy.

Neyah Wallace (6)
Moortown Primary School, Moortown

111

Roundhay Park

ℝ oundhay Park is a very big park

◎ ver the hills

𝕌 p and down

ℕ oisy ducks

𝔻 ads running around in Roundhay Park

ℍ aving great fun in Roundhay Park

𝔸 nd we have our lunch

𝕐 ou have to go to Roundhay Park

ℙ ark is noisy

𝔸 nd we play football

ℝ oundhay Park is a fun park

𝕂 ind people in the park.

Mansimar Singh
Moortown Primary School, Moortown

Roundhay Park

R ocks in the park.

O ver the hills.

U p and down the hills.

N ext we had our lunch.

D ogs barking in the park.

H appy people coming in the park.

A t Roundhay Park we like it the best.

Y oung children like Roundhay Park.

P ark is the best in the world.

A ll around us there are trees.

R unning in Roundhay Park makes me fit.

K eep the park clean and tidy.

Pavanpal Digpal
Moortown Primary School, Moortown

Roundhay Park

R unning around the park

O ver the hill in the park

U nder the trees it is dark

N oisy children in the park

D oing things in the park

H ow do you climb the trees?

A t the park it was fun

Y ucky - dog poo in the park

P laying in the park

A t the park we went on the roundabout

R ound and round on the roundabout

K eeping the dogs out of the park.

Maeve Richardson
Moortown Primary School, Moortown

Roundhay Park

R oundhay park is fun.

O ver the bumps.

U nder the tree there are boys and girls.

N ow we are running around.

D ogs are running around.

H ey, we are running!

A t lunch.

Y oung teenagers are running around.

P eople are running around.

A nd there are trees.

R oundhay is cool.

K eep the park clean!

Sami Jaber
Moortown Primary School, Moortown

Roundhay Park

R oundhay Park is fun.

O n that day we went

U p and down the hills.

N ow we are going.

D ucks swimming in the water.

H aving fun in the water.

A ll around us blue skies.

Y ummy ice cream.

P eople working.

A ll around us green grass.

R unning to keep you fit.

K eep you safe.

Holly Waddington
Moortown Primary School, Moortown

Friends

F riends are good to play with

R iding bikes is good to do with friends

I n your school you can play with your friends a lot

E ven if you fall out with your friends you will become friends again

N ever be nasty to your friends

D on't ever say names to your friends

S o that is my acrostic!

Jack Williams (7)
St John the Baptist Primary School, Leeds

Mathematics

M athematics is my favourite subject.

A dding you might do.

T ables you might learn.

H elp you might need.

E ventually it will get harder.

M aybe you will be a mathematician.

A dding: can you work out 222 + 444?

T ables: what is 6 x 6?

I think you should like it.

C an you work out what 111 + 111 equals?

S ubtract is another word for take away.

Rhianna Moore (7)
St John the Baptist Primary School, Leeds

Me

F atima is a good friend.

A pples are my favourite fruit.

T ennis my favourite sport.

' I n the Night Garden' is my favourite cartoon.

M y sister is good.

A t the park I play.

Fatima Shahzad (5)
Wakefield Girls' High School Junior School, Wakefield

119

Me

J oshua is my name.

O ranges are my favourite food.

S nakes are my favourite animals.

H ealthy things are good for you.

U nder my bed is a secret place.

A my is my friend.

Joshua Sheppard (5)
Wakefield Girls' High School Junior School, Wakefield

Me

H attie is a good friend

A nd I like chocolate

T ea is my favourite meal

T oday I am doing some writing

I like swimming

E lephants are my favourite animals.

Hattie Lloyd-Townshend (4)
Wakefield Girls' High School Junior School, Wakefield

Me

O livia is a good friend.

L oves lollipops.

I n the sun I am happy.

V egetables are my favourite.

I nside I play.

A lex is my friend.

Olivia Cole (5)
Wakefield Girls' High School Junior School, Wakefield

Me

S uzanne is kind.

U nicorns are my favourite.

Z ebras are black and white.

A nimals are my favourite.

N ew things are my favourite.

N eat I am.

E lephants are big.

Suzanne Brooke (5)
Wakefield Girls' High School Junior School, Wakefield

Me

A my is kind.

M y favourite shoes are red.

Y oghurts are very yummy.

Amy Deane (5)
Wakefield Girls' High School Junior School, Wakefield

Me

S arah is sensible

A nd she is smiling.

R abbits are my favourite

A nd I like dogs.

H orses are my favourite.

Sarah Selim (5)
Wakefield Girls' High School Junior School, Wakefield

Me

J oshua is very good to Tom.

O range is my favourite fruit.

S am is my friend.

H e is a good boy.

U nder my bed is my favourite hiding place,

A nd I am a big boy.

Joshua Morris (5)
Wakefield Girls' High School Junior School, Wakefield

Me

C harlie is kind.

H e is helpful,

A nd a good friend.

R obert is my middle name.

L ong is my go-kart.

I ride my bike.

E ggs are nice.

Charlie Paterson (5)
Wakefield Girls' High School Junior School, Wakefield

Holidays

H appy dolphins in the sea.

O livia is having a nice time on the sand.

L ucy is lost on the beach.

I love ice cream.

D ays at the seaside are fun.

A whale is diving in the sea.

Y esterday I saw a shark in the sea.

S avannah is running on the beach.

Lucy McKinlay (6)
Wakefield Girls' High School Junior School, Wakefield

Holidays

H appy days at the seaside.

O nly I am swimming in the sea.

L ovely squawking from the seagulls.

I love my beautiful ice cream.

D ads like diving in the waves.

A licia is talking to her friends.

Y esterday a young girl went to the beach.

S avannah is lying down on the towel.

Rio Paul Young (6)
Wakefield Girls' High School Junior School, Wakefield

Holidays

H appy, hot holidays are really fun.

O ne of the children is lost on the beach.

L emonade is lovely.

I love the seaside.

D ays pass by fast.

A ll the people are having a lovely time.

Y oung dogs love the beach.

S plashing in the sea is fun.

Guy Stuart-Brown (6)
Wakefield Girls' High School Junior School, Wakefield

Holidays

H appy times on the sandy beach.

O utdoors is fun on holidays.

L isten to the big waves.

I n and out of the ice cream shop.

D onkey rides that are really good.

A untie Sarah looking up at the seagulls.

Y esterday I went on a holiday.

S omeone's sunbathing in the sun.

Jacob Lonsdale (6)
Wakefield Girls' High School Junior School, Wakefield

Holidays

H ere we are at the beach!

O nly seagulls cry for food!

L ook at that dead fish!

I love donkey rides.

D addy's big waves!

A licia makes sandcastles.

Y ou are so wet!

S avannah loves ice cream!

Savannah Paris Young (6)
Wakefield Girls' High School Junior School, Wakefield

Holidays

H appy times on the beach.

O n the sand I run really fast.

L ollies are yummy.

I like the seaside.

D ads like swimming in the sea.

A licia likes ice cream.

Y our towel is getting really wet.

S avannah is listening to the seagulls.

Ella Jackman (6)
Wakefield Girls' High School Junior School, Wakefield

Holidays

H appy times on the beach.

O n the sand I run.

L isten to the seagulls squawk.

I t's lovely at the seaside.

D addies like to dive in the sea.

A mber likes ice lollies.

Y our beach mat is getting wet.

S indy and Sandy are sitting in the shade.

Amber Dosanjh (6)
Wakefield Girls' High School Junior School, Wakefield

Holidays

H ot days at the beach, what are we going to eat?

O ff I run to the sea.

L isten to the seagulls squawk.

I t's lovely at the seaside.

D ad dives in the water.

A way I go on the sand.

Y our feet are getting wet.

S ummer is great!

Jennifer Lin (5)
Wakefield Girls' High School Junior School, Wakefield

135

Holidays

H appy times at the wet beach.

O ne noisy time at the beach.

L isten to the seagulls.

I ce creams are yum-yum.

D ancing with the donkeys.

A licia likes ice creams.

Y esterday I saw a dolphin.

S tarfish are the best!

Alicia Love (6)
Wakefield Girls' High School Junior School, Wakefield

Holidays

H appy times on the beautiful beach.

O n the sand I build a sandcastle.

L isa swims in the great sea.

I ce creams are the best on the beach.

D ogs are not allowed on the beach.

A nnabel like the sandcastles.

Y esterday I went to the best beach.

S easides are the best!

Annabel Bond-Sampson (6)
Wakefield Girls' High School Junior School, Wakefield

Holidays

H opping on the sandy beach.

O utside I play in the sand.

L ovely hot dogs sizzling in the sun.

I love the beach.

D ads like the big waves.

A ll around you there is sand and water.

Y ellow sand between your toes.

S unbathing is great.

Alice Ives (6)
Wakefield Girls' High School Junior School, Wakefield

Holidays

H appy times at the beach.

O n the beach there are people.

L ovely cold lolly.

I nteresting seagulls fly around.

D onkey rides are fun.

A mazing sea to paddle in.

Y ellow sun shines on me.

S plashing dolphins in the sea.

Evie Wilson-Firth (6)
Wakefield Girls' High School Junior School, Wakefield

Holidays

H appy people on the beach.

O ne of the children is lost on the beach.

L isten to the seagulls squawk.

I love the beautiful beach.

D ancing dolphins in the sea.

A ll the people are having a fantastic time at the seaside.

Y achts sail in the sea.

S un is hot on the sandy beach.

Luke Hutchinson (6)
Wakefield Girls' High School Junior School, Wakefield

Holidays

H appy times on the beautiful beach.

O n the sand I race my sister.

L isten to the sea waves crash the rocks.

I like to listen to the seagulls squawk.

D addy is daydreaming on the beach.

A untie is looking for seagulls.

Y our beach towel is getting wet.

S omeone is sunbathing near a cave.

Oliver Hulse (6)
Wakefield Girls' High School Junior School, Wakefield

141

Holidays

Happy holidays are really fun.

Only seagulls cry for food.

Look at that dead fish!

I love ice cream.

Daddy likes playing and so do I.

A seagull searches on the sandy beach.

You and me went to a cave.

Splashing in the waves.

Tom Preece (6)
Wakefield Girls' High School Junior School, Wakefield

Holidays

H appy times on the beach.

O n the sand I run.

L isten to the seagulls squawk.

I like to jump in the water.

D ads like to swim in the water.

A t the beach I like ice cream.

Y our beach mat is getting wet.

S avannah is lying on the towel.

Joshua Smith (6)
Wakefield Girls' High School Junior School, Wakefield

I Am . . .

A njali is a nice person to play with

N ever talks in class

J ust a little shy

A good reader

L ikes chicken

I like bikes

N ever tells fibs

A wonderful person

R eally wants a pet

E very day works hard

N ot very keen on football

D oesn't eat bananas

R eally good at art

A nd very smart

N ice to know.

Anjali Narendran (6)
Wakefield Girls' High School Junior School, Wakefield

I Am . . .

A nisha is fun and creative, she is not

N aughty at home or at school.

I have two brothers.

S ome people run faster than me. I

H elp people in their work

A nd I do not have a sister.

K ind and caring to people.

A nisha is Alex's best friend.

M y birthday is in March

A nd I have pet fish. I always

T ry to work my best.

H appy all the time.

Anisha Kamath (7)
Wakefield Girls' High School Junior School, Wakefield

I Am . . .

A mai is nice and fun.

M onkey tricks in a hand,

A nd likes to join in a marching band.

I mpatient to eat ice cream.

G oing to the beach,

A nd loves to eat a peach.

N othing stops to make me bad.

J am makes you a healthy lad.

A lways helps friends.

M akes big changes to the ends.

Amai Ganjam (7)
Wakefield Girls' High School Junior School, Wakefield

146

I Am

A lex is fun and kind.

L ikes reading books lots.

E xciting games all the time.

X -ray needed when I broke my leg,

A nd I have a sister.

N ice and creative.

D rawing I really like to do.

R ude I am not.

A lex is cute.

M y sister has curly hair.

I like to swim.

D o not have a brother.

D o have a fish.

L ots of friends I have at school

E at lots of food I do.

T ry to work my best.

O ctober is my birthday.

N ice and kind all the time.

Alexandra Middleton (7)
Wakefield Girls' High School Junior School, Wakefield

I Am . . .

A t all times I am cheeky.

D on't go near me, I am so cheeky.

R acing is my favourite thing to do.

I ce cream is my favourite.

E xcellent work from me.

N ice, shiny, sparkly jewellery fit for a lady like me.

N ice ice lollies that are my favourites.

E veryone looks up to me.

I am an intelligent girl.

V iews are my favourite things to see on top of mountains.

E ating lots of healthy food makes me helpful.

S ports are my favourite things to do.

Adrienne Ives (6)
Wakefield Girls' High School Junior School, Wakefield

I Am . . .

S ophie, yes me, I'm cheeky

O h I am cheeky

P utting chewing gum on the chair

H ey, I told you I'm cheeky!

I have a hedgehog

E ven I've fed it

W hat, I've forgotten something

A nd my DS

I n and out of the house

N ow are we ready?

W ell yes we are

R eady . . . off we go

I n the car, we can't wait

' G o faster!' I said

' H ow long is it

T ill we get there?'

Sophie Wainwright (7)
Wakefield Girls' High School Junior School, Wakefield

I Am . . .

R euben is

E xcellent on the computer

U know he is cool

B en is my best friend

E mily is mad

N ice to Daniel

W ill is the tallest

A mai is jokey

L uke is running

K ey is being clever

E veryone's friend

R ugby and football are the best.

Reuben Walker (7)
Wakefield Girls' High School Junior School, Wakefield

I Am . . .

D aniel is

A really good football player

N ot good at board games

I like dogs

E specially

L ike playing off-ground tig.

M y best friend is really funny

C atch with my dad is real fun

N ice with people

A good aimer at throwing

I 'm especially good at hiding

R euben is my best friend.

Daniel McNair (7)
Wakefield Girls' High School Junior School, Wakefield

151

I Am . . .

E lla likes reading books

L ollipops are my favourite sweets

L ovely and beautiful

A really nice friend to other people

C ares for everyone, especially my best friends

R unning is fun

A lovely summer's day to wear a dress

V ases of sweet peas in my bedroom make it smell nice

E specially my best friend Emily too

N ice little girl.

Ella Craven (7)
Wakefield Girls' High School Junior School, Wakefield

I Am . . .

E verybody loves me in my family
M y pets are soft and cute
I am so fashionable
L aughter is my favourite subject
Y ears ago I was born

S wimming is my favourite sport
U nable to roller skate but learning
T ime by time I get older
C urly and brown hair
L ots of times I play with my dolls
I am cheeky
F abulous work
F avourite food is strawberries
E mily is my name.

Emily Sutcliffe (7)
Wakefield Girls' High School Junior School, Wakefield

153

I Am . . .

E verybody plays with me.

M olly is one of my friends.

M aha skips with me.

A nisha plays with me a bit.

A manda is my mum.

S ophie plays with me in early morning club.

H all is my last name.

T omorrow I am going to school.

O n the weekend I am going to Scotland.

N eat I am.

H ate to see disgusting people.

A nts are one of my favourite pets.

L ibby is my very best friend.

L ovely, sweet, cute and neat I am.

Emma Ashton Hall (7)
Wakefield Girls' High School Junior School, Wakefield

I Am . . .

E ve likes school a lot

V ery excited to see what they've got

E veryone can be my friend

W ell not always till the end

I want to be helpful and say

'C an I help you?'

K icking balls and dancing I like too

H ave you got any teddy bears? I have

A bsolutely loads and they all love me

M y family, I have three brothers, 1, 2, 3 . . .

Eve Wickham (7)
Wakefield Girls' High School Junior School, Wakefield

I Am . . .

G eorgia likes apples.

E very year I get older.

O ften I sit in my room and draw.

R unning is fun.

G eorgia likes to sleep in.

I n my room I have a double bed.

A nd I like eating a lot.

N ow I have two horses and one pony in my field.

U se fun things every day.

T ime by time I grow.

T ime by time I get better at things

A nd I like chickens.

L ots and lots of playing in the garden.

L ots of times I wrestle my brother.

Georgia Nuttall (7)
Wakefield Girls' High School Junior School, Wakefield

I Am . . .

L aurence goes to karate

A lways hungry

U nable to roller skate

R eally good at video games

E ven better than my dad

N ice to my friends

C lever at maths

E specially adding quickly

H ate getting changed for PE

A lways listening

R eally likes to read

K ind to everyone

I like swimming

N ever rude to adults.

Laurence Harkin (7)
Wakefield Girls' High School Junior School, Wakefield

I Am . . .

L ovely Libby

I like Emma and Ruby, they're my best friends

B ut I like to be healthy

B ut I love to keep fit

Y ears go by and I get older

M y sister is called Darcy

A nice dinner tonight, I hope

Y oung and sweet

O ops, I forget my teddy!

Libby Mayo (7)
Wakefield Girls' High School Junior School, Wakefield

My First Acrostic – Leeds & Wakefield

I Am . . .

L illie is fun and creative all the time.

I ce lollies are Lillie's favourite food.

L illie loves horse riding.

L illie is six years old.

I magination is in Lillie's mind.

E veryone looks up to Lillie.

J ones is my last name.

O h Lillie is so silly.

N ever is Lillie bad.

E xciting news comes from Lillie.

S he is helpful at all times.

Lillie Jones (6)
Wakefield Girls' High School Junior School, Wakefield

I Am . . .

M y sister is the best at playing.

A big person like my brother likes playing with me.

H annah is my favourite person who sings.

A lways like to play on the swings because it makes me happy.

N ice people like me play with each other.

A person of two are friends.

S ay nice things to your friends they will be playing with you.

E ven I have a tree house in my back garden.

E verybody likes me in my family.

M y mummy is the best at working, she makes nice food.

Maha Naseem (6)
Wakefield Girls' High School Junior School, Wakefield

I Am . . .

M y name is Megan Morris

E veryone thinks I am fun

G orgeous and pretty

A nd my parents are lovely

N ice I am and everyone thinks so

M y mum is called Siobhan and my dad, John

O h I love my teacher so much

R ude children I don't like

I hate to leave my teacher

S o I'm a very nice person.

Megan Morris (7)
Wakefield Girls' High School Junior School, Wakefield

I Am . . .

Mostly I like to write.

Often I like to read.

Lots of flowers in the garden.

Lots of time with friends.

Years go by and I get older, I like it.

But I like to keep fit.

Oh I am clumsy.

Use fun things every day.

Look at the sun.

Try to drink.

Oops I always forget my teddies.

Never forget to water the flowers.

Molly Boulton (6)
Wakefield Girls' High School Junior School, Wakefield

I Am . . .

O ctober is not my birthday.

L ove is a gift.

I adore zebras.

V elvet is the favourite part of my dress.

I do not have two sisters.

A n apple is red.

W oods are scary.

O livia is my name.

O h I left the cookies in the kitchen.

D ogs I will get.

H ats I wear to school.

E nd of school year I hate.

A dog would be nice.

D addy is called Mark.

Olivia Woodhead (6)
Wakefield Girls' High School Junior School, Wakefield

I Am . . .

O rganised

L unatic

I maginative

V olunteer

I nfant

A dventurous.

Olivia Smith (7)
Wakefield Girls' High School Junior School, Wakefield

I Am . . .

F eeling funky

R apping, rumbling

E ating eggs

Y apping, yelling

A lways admiring.

Freya Allatt (7)
Wakefield Girls' High School Junior School, Wakefield

I Am . . .

J am is yummy

O wls are amazing

A mazing at running

N ever be horrible

N aughty at homework

A palling shouter.

Joanna Fearnehough (7)
Wakefield Girls' High School Junior School, Wakefield

I Am . . .

F ootball final.

I ntelligent skills.

N ice boy, man

N eat, strong man.

Finn O'Gara (7)
Wakefield Girls' High School Junior School, Wakefield

I Am . . .

A mazing at running

D oing football is my best hobby

A mazing at long jump

M agnificent at football.

Adam Marwood (7)
Wakefield Girls' High School Junior School, Wakefield

I Am . . .

G ood at rugby

E xcellent boy

O n and on I'm really good

R eally good

G ood at football

E xcellent at maths.

George Jones (7)
Wakefield Girls' High School Junior School, Wakefield

I Am . . .

R espectful and funny.

A very funny girl.

C ounting is lots of fun.

H alves are interesting.

E xercise is fun.

L ikes ice cream.

Rachel Simister (6)
Wakefield Girls' High School Junior School, Wakefield

I Am . . .

R osalind is my name.

O utside I love playing, I have lots of fun.

S un is wonderful, it shines and shines.

A nimals are wonderful.

L over of animals am I.

I love to play.

N ew Zealand is so hot.

D ad's name is Gordon.

Rosalind Maddan (7)
Wakefield Girls' High School Junior School, Wakefield

I Am . . .

Y es I am the best at cricket.

O n TV the best thing to watch is cricket.

U nbeatable Yousaf.

S uper Yousaf.

A mazing Yousaf.

F ootball is the best thing to play.

Yousaf Shahzad (7)
Wakefield Girls' High School Junior School, Wakefield

I Am . . .

O ctober is a fun month

L oving Mum, Dad and brother

I love cuddling my little brother

V iolent and adventurous

E ight rugby matches a day

R ugby, I love rugby.

Oliver Farrar (7)
Wakefield Girls' High School Junior School, Wakefield

I Am . . .

I ntelligent girl

S illy sometimes

O utside girl

B eautiful lady

E nergetic at times

L aughing a lot.

Isobel Taylor (7)
Wakefield Girls' High School Junior School, Wakefield

My First Acrostic - Leeds & Wakefield

I Am . . .

M aths is fun

A mazing intelligent boy

T oo good to miss

T ennis is fantastic

H appy smiling boy

E nglish is nice

W onderful.

Matthew Wood (6)
Wakefield Girls' High School Junior School, Wakefield

I Am . . .

I ce cream is lovely

M um is very kind

O livia is very kind

G uitars are cool

E lephants are big

N urses are intelligent.

Imogen Birch-Dixon (7)
Wakefield Girls' High School Junior School, Wakefield

I Am . . .

W ants to play football very much

I gnores bad things

L ikes to play any boy game

L ikes to do the same as others

I will do anything for my friends

A nd I will be patient for chocolate

M y mum and dad are very nice and caring
and my sister and brother are very sharing

J uggles a lot

O ctopuses are my favourite animal

Y ellow is my worst colour

C andy is my favourite treat

E xcellent at maths.

William Joyce (7)
Wakefield Girls' High School Junior School, Wakefield

I Am . . .

T otally tremendous at art.

O utrageous in different ways

B onkers on my bike.

I ntelligent in maths.

Tobi Irelewuyi (7)
Wakefield Girls' High School Junior School, Wakefield

I Am . . .

O livia is kind

L oves animals

I mogen is my best friend

V iolet is my favourite colour

I love to sing

A Victorian trip was my favourite trip.

Olivia Pye (7)
Wakefield Girls' High School Junior School, Wakefield

179

I Am . . .

E aster she likes the best.

L ikes to go to Spain.

L oves to dance.

A very nice girl.

Ella Northern (6)
Wakefield Girls' High School Junior School, Wakefield

I Am . . .

K icking is a hobby!

A bsolutely great at falling over!

T op at art!

E nglish is good!

Kate Armstrong (7)
Wakefield Girls' High School Junior School, Wakefield

I Am . . .

A pril is my favourite month.

I mogen is a good friend.

M y mum is very kind.

E xcellent work today.

E xpecting a kind friend.

Aimee Rose Blake (7)
Wakefield Girls' High School Junior School, Wakefield

I Am . . .

A mazing roller coasters and rides!

N ice dancing and writing.

S oft skin and sensible.

H onest and helpful little girl.

I ntelligent girl at handwriting and English.

N oisy night person.

I ndoor and outdoor type of person, likes playing cricket.

Anshini Thakur (7)
Wakefield Girls' High School Junior School, Wakefield

I Am . . .

S uper girl in English sometimes.

O riginal girl.

P eaceful girl all the time.

H iding from her daddy all the time.

I ntelligent girl in English.

E xciting girl for parties and going to people's houses.

Sophie Knowles (7)
Wakefield Girls' High School Junior School, Wakefield

Me

M ax plays

A nya watches

I sabella counts

S even sweets

I shopped

E mily cried.

Maisie McMillan (4)
Wakefield Girls' High School Junior School, Wakefield

Me

E mily plays

L illy watches

I zzy counts to ten

Z ibb counts to 100

A nisha cries

B ibee comes to play

E lla comes to play

T he sister cries

H appy holiday.

Elizabeth Haigh (5)
Wakefield Girls' High School Junior School, Wakefield

Me

H e plays with me

A nisha goes shopping

R eshmina counts seven sweets

R ose went to get an apple

I went to go for a sleepover

E mily went to the shop to get a cake

T o Grandma, love from Harriet.

Harriet Greenwood (5)
Wakefield Girls' High School Junior School, Wakefield

Me

I sabella Cried

S he played at my house

A nya does shopping

B ronte helps me tidy my room

E van plays with me

L et's be special.

Isabel Ramsden (5)
Wakefield Girls' High School Junior School, Wakefield

Me

A nisha acted like a clown

N ow my sister is a toddler

I s Harriet shopping?

S it on the chair

H arriet plays with me

A nya rides on her horse.

Anisha Ahir (5)
Wakefield Girls' High School Junior School, Wakefield

Me

E mily cried

M aisie came to play

I sabella counts seven sweets

L ots of people

Y ummy, Yummy!

Emily Greenwood (5)
Wakefield Girls' High School Junior School, Wakefield

Me

E mily plays

V ans came to the football pitches

A nya counts ten sweets

N o more sweets!

Evan Clark (5)
Wakefield Girls' High School Junior School, Wakefield

Me

E mily plays

L ove Mum

L ovely pop

A n apple

S it on

H eavy ball

A fraid Ella

W alk tall.

Ella Shaw (5)
Wakefield Girls' High School Junior School, Wakefield

Me

R ide my bike

E mily cried

S even sweets on the table

H arriet is nice

M ax plays football

I sabel is Evan's friend

N anny came

A pples are yum.

Reshmina Naseem (5)
Wakefield Girls' High School Junior School, Wakefield

Me

I 've got a teddy called Boo.

S o can we all go the park.

A nya plays with me.

B oo smells really bad.

E lla's coming to my house.

L illie is coming to my house.

L ucy is my friend.

A nya plays with my watch.

Isabella Rust (4)
Wakefield Girls' High School Junior School, Wakefield

194

Me

E lizabeth is very kind

L ikes fascinating animals

I s a good best friend

Z oe is her friend

A beaming smile

B eautiful

E xcellent

T ries hard

H elpful person.

Elizabeth Kate Sykes (5)
Wakefield Girls' High School Junior School, Wakefield

Me

Zoos are my favourite.

Ostriches I love.

Elephants I love.

My brother is Sam.

Everyone I love.

Rabbits I love.

Everton is my favourite football team.

Daddy is lovely.

I love Mum.

Trains are my favourite ride.

Hats are lovely.

Zoe Meredith (5)
Wakefield Girls' High School Junior School, Wakefield

Me

E leanor is fabulous.

L ikes yellow and fascinating animals.

E leanor is good.

A lways is nice.

N ever kicks.

O nly eats healthy food.

R eads really well.

Eleanor Bowen (5)
Wakefield Girls' High School Junior School, Wakefield

Me

J ack likes jelly.

A lways fabulous at writing.

C haotic is my favourite game.

K arate might be fun.

Jack Young (5)
Wakefield Girls' High School Junior School, Wakefield

Me

A melia is very kind.

M y best friends are Holly and Elizabeth.

E very day I come to school.

L ater I go home.

I s very happy.

A melia always works hard.

Amelia Wormald (5)
Wakefield Girls' High School Junior School, Wakefield

Me

H annah is beautiful.

A lways smiling.

N ever sad.

N ever cries.

A lways does good work.

H elps everybody.

Hannah Wilson (5)
Wakefield Girls' High School Junior School, Wakefield

Me

A aron is a good tackler at footie

A aron is a good writer

R unning is his exercise

O ver in the playground

N ow I am writing.

Aaron Dyer (5)
Wakefield Girls' High School Junior School, Wakefield

Me

H olly is very kind.

O nly plays with Grandad.

L ovely fairy.

L ovely princess.

Y ou are special.

Holly Rusling (5)
Wakefield Girls' High School Junior School, Wakefield

Me

R ohan is good.

O ver he jumps in the playground.

H e likes playing.

A good football player.

N ew stickers too.

Rohan Bhimsaria (5)
Wakefield Girls' High School Junior School, Wakefield

Me

A lexandra is always kind to Jemima and Olivia H.

L ikes puzzles.

E leanor and Zoe are her friends.

X xxx to Daddy, love from Alexandra!

Alexandra Parkes (5)
Wakefield Girls' High School Junior School, Wakefield

Holidays

H oliday time is here.

O n the plane I get, after

L oading the car.

I love it!

D ad took us swimming. It's

A lovely day to go to the beach

Y es we're here. It is

S o sunny here.

Jessie Evans (5)
Wakefield Girls' High School Junior School, Wakefield

Holidays

H ot sun

O range juice for me

L ovely day

I had an ice cream

D addy went on the donkey ride

A nd I went in the sea

Y esterday I was in the sun

S unny days.

Natasha Boden (6)
Wakefield Girls' High School Junior School, Wakefield

Holidays

H ooray it's holiday time!

O h I go high over the sea.

L ilos are the best thing I liked!

I 'm always hot on my holidays.

D addy lets me have an ice cream.

A fter I've had my ice cream I have a swim.

Y esterday I went to the seaside.

S easides are very hot.

Ebony Cottam (6)
Wakefield Girls' High School Junior School, Wakefield

Holidays

H ot dog to eat in the sun

O range juice to drink

L ollipops to lick

I ce lollies to make

D onkey rides for a treat

A eroplanes make lines in the sky

Y esterday was the best day

S wimming in the sea.

Temi Irelewuyi (6)
Wakefield Girls' High School Junior School, Wakefield

Holidays

H ooray it's holiday.

O ff to the airport we go.

L oading the car.

I nside the car we go.

D riving along the road we go.

A long, along we go

Y es we're there wow, it's

S o sunny here!

Amy Scott (6)
Wakefield Girls' High School Junior School, Wakefield

Holidays

H olidays are exciting.

O nly one can go on the trampoline. I

L ove this, don't you?

I t's a sunny day.

D o you want to go to the beach?

A fter tea we go to the shop.

Y esterday I went to the pool.

S ummer is nice!

Rosie Higgins (6)
Wakefield Girls' High School Junior School, Wakefield

Holidays

H ot dog for a treat

O ctopus lives underwater

L icking lollipops

I ce cream around my face

D onkeys having a race

A eroplanes flying

Y achts are floating

S cuba-diving in the sea.

Stevan Opacic (6)
Wakefield Girls' High School Junior School, Wakefield

Holidays

H ot sun on my back when I'm on the beach.

O ctopus under the sea

L ollipops to lick.

I ce in my drink.

D onkey rides on the beach.

A eroplane in the sky.

Y esterday was sunny.

S andcastles to build.

Sadie Pitts (6)
Wakefield Girls' High School Junior School, Wakefield

Holidays

H olidays are the best.

O h we are going swimming.

L ike to play, Sam?

I am swimming in the sea.

D o you want to play with the ball?

A boy was playing volleyball.

Y ay it's holidays. The

S easide is sunny!

Matthew Deighan (6)
Wakefield Girls' High School Junior School, Wakefield

Holidays

H ot at the seaside

O n the beach

L ollipops

I deas for sandcastles

D igging holes in the sand

A fish in the sea

Y achts on the sea

S un in the sky.

Matthew Ainley (6)
Wakefield Girls' High School Junior School, Wakefield

Holidays

H olidays are the best!

O n holiday I get ice cream. I

L ove the sunshine!

I love the beach.

D addy swims in the water

A nd I did a backwards roly-poly.

Y esterday I saw a crab. I love

S unny weather and holidays!

Grace Herrington (6)
Wakefield Girls' High School Junior School, Wakefield

Holidays

H ooray it's the holiday. I

O nly pack my stuff. I

L ove going on holiday by plane.

I love it because it is exciting.

D ad always goes to sleep.

A n aeroplane goes very, very fast.

Y esterday I was on the beach.

S o when we got there I built sandcastles.

Oliver Butterfield (5)
Wakefield Girls' High School Junior School, Wakefield

Holidays

H ooray it's holiday time.

O h I go high over the sea. I

L ove the seaside.

I 'm always hot on boats.

D addy always gets me chocolate.

A fter I get an ice cream too.

Y esterday we went

S wimming as it was sunny!

Felicity Hutchinson (6)
Wakefield Girls' High School Junior School, Wakefield

Holidays

H ooray it's the holidays.

O n holiday, every day I go swimming.

L ovely holidays are here.

I love going on holiday.

D addy eats an ice cream on holiday.

A Spanish lady dances on stage.

'Y um-yum,' said Daddy when he ate the ice cream.

S ometimes my family come on holiday.

Daiya Shergill (6)
Wakefield Girls' High School Junior School, Wakefield

Holidays

H ooray it's the holidays.

O n holiday it's hot.

L ovely holidays are fun.

I like swimming in the sea.

D oes our lilo float?

A fter our train ride we're going swimming.

Y esterday the sun was very hot.

S o after the exciting day we have a rest.

Alice Clibbens (6)
Wakefield Girls' High School Junior School, Wakefield

Holidays

H ooray holidays are here!

O n the plane I go, I can see the clouds.

L ook at the sun!

I love going on holiday,

D ad is at home doing the cleaning!

A nd we're having fun on holiday!

Y esterday we went to the beach.

S unday was hot.

Lauren McCormack (6)
Wakefield Girls' High School Junior School, Wakefield

Holidays

H appy holidays!

O n holiday we go on aeroplanes!

L ike swimming in pools. I jump in!

I like ice cream sometimes.

D o go for a dive in the pool now,

A nd have a nice time.

Y ou can swim with me.

S untan cream on, now I can play!

Charlotte Lloyd-Townshend (6)
Wakefield Girls' High School Junior School, Wakefield

Holidays

H olidays are great when you get there.

O h how I love to go on the beach

L ying on the sun bench and sunbathing.

I splash my mum on the side.

D ay after day I swim in the pool.

A n ice cream van came by.

Y esterday I had a go at

S panish dancing in Spain.

Alanis Milner-Moore (6)
Wakefield Girls' High School Junior School, Wakefield

Holidays

H ooray it is a hot day.

O ne day I went to the swimming pool.

L ook at the sea.

I had an ice cream on the beach.

D id you build a sandcastle?

A fter I went in the car.

Y esterday I went on a train.

S unday, I went on the beach.

Emily Greenough (5)
Wakefield Girls' High School Junior School, Wakefield

Me

O livia is good at writing

L oves the leaves that blow off the trees.

I s very beautiful

V ery good

I s super kind

A lways smiles.

Olivia Hargill (5)
Wakefield Girls' High School Junior School, Wakefield

Me

J ames is jolly.

A lways brings good toys.

M akes a mess.

E ats chocolate.

S its on a chair.

James Butterfield (5)
Wakefield Girls' High School Junior School, Wakefield

Me

E lla is a good writer.

L eia is her sister.

L ikes to be Cinderella.

A pples are her favourite snack.

Ella Boote (5)
Wakefield Girls' High School Junior School, Wakefield

Me

A lexander is good at reading

L ikes playing

E ats pasta

X xxx for Mum.

Alexander Allen (4)
Wakefield Girls' High School Junior School, Wakefield

Holidays

H is for having a smashing time

O makes me think of eating octopus

L is for looking at the stars

I is for using your imagination

D reminds me of dozing in the sun

A makes me think of acrobats in August

Y is for yummy food

S is for smashing, sizzling barbecues!

Anna Chew (6)
Wakefield Girls' High School Junior School, Wakefield

Holidays

H is for having a good time

O is for octopus

L is for licking lollipops

I is for insect spray

D is for dodgems

A is for accidents

Y is for yellow sun

S is for sandy sandcastles.

Lucy Assassa (6)
Wakefield Girls' High School Junior School, Wakefield

229

Holidays

H is for the holidays.

O is for jumping over the waves.

L is for lying.

I is for having an ice cream.

D is for diving in the sea.

A is for a seagull.

Y is for yachts.

S is for the salty sea.

Luca Zammuto (6)
Wakefield Girls' High School Junior School, Wakefield

Holidays

H is for having a good time

O makes me think of the opera

L is for licking lollipops

I is for nice ice cream

D is for the dodgem cars

A is for acrobats in August

Y is for the yellow sand

S is for sunbathing.

Aamer Khan (6)
Wakefield Girls' High School Junior School, Wakefield

231

Holidays

H is for hiding behind the sandcastles.

O is for opening an ice lolly packet.

L is for lazy people lying on the beach.

I is for the icy cold sea.

D is for dolphins in the sea.

A is for ants on the sand.

Y is for yummy ice creams.

S is for the green seaweed.

Harriet Ostrowski Jones (6)
Wakefield Girls' High School Junior School, Wakefield

Holidays

H is for Harriet having a happy time.

O reminds me of obeying the safety rules.

L is for lying in the sun.

I makes me think of ice skating.

D is for diving in the sea.

A is for Alex splashing in the sea.

Y is for the yellow sun.

S is for seaside.

Teaghan Murphy (6)
Wakefield Girls' High School Junior School, Wakefield

Holidays

H reminds me of happy days

O is for jumping over the waves in the sea

L makes me think of lying in the sun

I is for ice cream

D reminds me of Daddy's sunburn

A is for adoring the views

Y is for the yellow sun

S makes me think of splashing in the sea.

Leighton Shuttleworth (6)
Wakefield Girls' High School Junior School, Wakefield

Holidays

H is for having a good time.

O is for obeying the safety rules.

L is for lying in the sun.

I is for eating ice lollies.

D is for riding a donkey.

A is for Anna in the sea.

Y is for yellow sun.

S is for making a snowman.

Millie Evans (6)
Wakefield Girls' High School Junior School, Wakefield

Holidays

H iding in the sand dunes.

O is for jumping over the waves.

L icking the lollipops.

I ce cream.

D is for donkeys.

A is for adoring the views.

Y ellow sun.

S is for splashing.

Felicity Milner (6)
Wakefield Girls' High School Junior School, Wakefield

Holidays

H is for having hot dogs

O is for jumping over the waves.

L is for licking lollipops.

I is for having an ice lolly.

D is for diving in the sea.

A is for adoring the views.

Y is for your imagination.

S is for splashing in the sea.

James Binney (6)
Wakefield Girls' High School Junior School, Wakefield

Holidays

H iding in the sand dunes.

O is for jumping over the waves.

L icking lollipops.

I ce cream

D iving in the sea.

A ccidents.

Y ellow sun.

S is for hot sun.

James Barker (6)
Wakefield Girls' High School Junior School, Wakefield

Holidays

H is for the hot yellow sun.

O is for the octopus.

L is for licking a lollipop.

I is for eating an ice cream.

D is for daddies sunbathing.

A is for Anna in the sea.

Y is for the yellow sand.

S is for splashing in the waves.

Lucy Cockayne (5)
Wakefield Girls' High School Junior School, Wakefield

Holidays

H is for having hot dogs.

O is for obeying the safety rules.

L is for listening to the lifeguards.

I is for ice cream.

D is for diving in the sea.

A is for an aquarium.

Y is for yummy food.

S is for smelly seaweed.

Huda Chowdhery (6)
Wakefield Girls' High School Junior School, Wakefield

Holidays

H is for having a good time.

O is for obeying the safety rules.

L is for lying in the sun.

I is for ice lollies.

D is for riding donkeys.

A is for adoring the view.

Y ellow sun.

S is for splashing.

Holly Dyson (6)
Wakefield Girls' High School Junior School, Wakefield

Holidays

H is for having fun.

O is for obeying rules.

L is for licking lollies.

I is for imagination.

D is for donkey rides.

A is for admiring views.

Y is for yellow yacht.

S is for sniffing the seaside smells.

Joseph Gueli (6)
Wakefield Girls' High School Junior School, Wakefield

I Am . . .

H issing at my cat.

A crobatics is what I like best.

R unning is what I like.

R ugby is what I do.

I love dancing.

E njoy reading and

T asks that are hard.

Harriet!

Harriet Liley (6)
Wakefield Girls' High School Junior School, Wakefield

I Am . . .

S o nice to animals.

O ften riding horses.

F ish are my favourite pets.

I like to play with my friends.

A rt is my favourite subject.

Sofia!

Sofia Guilherme (7)
Wakefield Girls' High School Junior School, Wakefield

I Am . . .

O beying people all the time.

L oves eating sweets!

I love to play.

V ery clever at science.

I am polite all the time.

A lways asking good questions.

Olivia!

Olivia Wilson (7)
Wakefield Girls' High School Junior School, Wakefield

I Am . . .

J olly all the time

O bstacle courses rule to me

S upports Manchester United all the time

H ides a lot of times

U nbelievably messy all the time.

A ction all the time in my house.

Joshua!

Joshua Charnock (7)
Wakefield Girls' High School Junior School, Wakefield

I Am . . .

K een on tennis.

E nemies are bad to me.

S piders are scared of me.

H aving love for my brother.

A pples are tasty to me.

V ideos are nice to watch for me.

Keshav!

Keshav Nair (7)
Wakefield Girls' High School Junior School, Wakefield

247

I Am . . .

R uby's work is untidy

U mbrellas keep me dry

B eing kind all the time

Y ellow is my favourite colour.

Ruby!

Ruby Joffe (6)
Wakefield Girls' High School Junior School, Wakefield

My First Acrostic - Leeds & Wakefield

I Am . . .

L oves butter.

O ften plays with Katie.

U nder a sun umbrella is where I love to be.

I love cuddling Cutie, my guinea pig.

S cared of spiders.

A lways chatting!

Louisa!

Louisa Hutchinson (6)
Wakefield Girls' High School Junior School, Wakefield

I Am . . .

J azz music is cool.

A sleep a lot.

S weets I eat on Friday.

M ilk I drink at night.

I ce cream I get when we go out.

N ecklaces I wear.

E ating rice pudding I love.

Jasmine!

Jasmine Caddies (7)
Wakefield Girls' High School Junior School, Wakefield

My First Acrostic - Leeds & Wakefield

I Am . . .

K ite - flying in the wind.

A t home lying down in bed.

T ennis makes me fit.

I n and out of the snow.

E njoying Mrs Stainsby's stories.

Katie!

Katie Appleyard (7)
Wakefield Girls' High School Junior School, Wakefield

I Am . . .

J ogging in the playground.

A rt is very good.

M eeting for the football game.

E xercise is good in PE.

S almon is good to eat.

James!

James Parkinson (7)
Wakefield Girls' High School Junior School, Wakefield

I Am . . .

S upports Manchester United.

A nd I play football with my friends.

M atches are good because I save some goals.

Sam!

Sam Meredith (6)
Wakefield Girls' High School Junior School, Wakefield

I Am . . .

M anchester United is my best team.

I like eating ice cream.

H aving a great football team,

A nd I play football with my friends.

L earning is fun.

I love animals.

Mihali!

Mihali Joannou (7)
Wakefield Girls' High School Junior School, Wakefield

I Am . . .

A rt is my favourite.

L ove ladybirds.

E njoy listening to Mrs Stainsby's stories.

X -rays are interesting.

Alex!

Alexandra Dyer (7)
Wakefield Girls' High School Junior School, Wakefield

I Am . . .

A rt is my favourite thing.

M onday is science day.

E njoy doing maths.

L earn to be clever.

I ce cream is lovely.

A ccurate verbs is what I do.

Amelia!

Amelia Penfold (6)
Wakefield Girls' High School Junior School, Wakefield

I Am . . .

E njoys art.

I really like ice hockey.

L oves dogs.

I like ice cream.

D affodils are my favourite flowers.

H oops are my favourite toy.

Eilidh!

Eilidh Lee (6)
Wakefield Girls' High School Junior School, Wakefield

I Am . . .

Games are good, I like playing on them.

Exercise makes me fit.

Oasis is a good drink.

' Ruby' is a good song.

Galaxy chocolate is my favourite chocolate.

Everything I see is interesting.

George!

George Purves-Bennett (7)
Wakefield Girls' High School Junior School, Wakefield

My First Acrostic - Leeds & Wakefield

I Am . . .

S paghetti I love

E ating fruit I love

E van eating vegetables

T ickling my daddy and teddy bears

A lways drinking water

L icking lovely lollipops.

Seetal!

Seetal Patel (7)
Wakefield Girls' High School Junior School, Wakefield

I Am . . .

T rips are cool.

I like dogs.

A lligators scare me!

    Tia!

Tia Long (7)
Wakefield Girls' High School Junior School, Wakefield